SPECIAL
DAYS
AF595801
ANZAC DAY
JANE PFEIFFER
REDBACK
publishing

First published 2023 by
Redback Publishing
Suite 6, 13a Narabang Way,
Belrose NSW 2085
Australia

www.redbackpublishing.com
orders@redbackpublishing.com

©Redback Publishing 2023
Reprinted 2026

ISBN 978-1-761400-22-3

Author: Jane Pfeiffer
Editor: Caroline Thomas
Design: Redback Publishing

Original illustrations © Redback Publishing 2023
Originated by Redback Publishing

Every effort has been made to contact copyright holders of any material reproduced in this book. Any omissions will be rectified in subsequent printings if notice is given to the publisher.

Disclaimer
All the internet addresses (URLs) given in this book were valid at the time of going to press. However, due to the dynamic nature of the internet, some addresses may have changed, or sites may have changed or ceased to exist since publication. While the author and publisher regret any inconvenience this may cause readers, no responsibility for any such changes can be accepted by either the author or the publisher.

Acknowledgements
Abbreviations: l—left, r—right, b—bottom, t—top, c—centre, m—middle
We would like to thank the following for permission to reproduce photographs: (Images © shutterstock, wikimediacommons) p11br ArliftAtoz2205, p12mr Maneerat Shotiyanpitak , p14br Adwo, p15tl GTS Productions, p16cm GTS Productions, p18cm Sue Martin, p18bl olddong , p19br Milleflore Images, p19cm paintings, p20cm Ankit M, p22-23 Neale Cousland, p25br paintings, p28mr Gordon Best, p29bl olddong, p30mr Milleflore Images

Copyright Statement
All rights reserved. No part of this publication may be reproduced in any form or by any means (including photocopying or storing it in any medium by electronic means and whether or not transiently or incidentally to some other use of this publication) without the written permission of the copyright owner. Applications for the copyright owner's written permission should be addressed to the publisher.

A catalogue record for this book is available from the National Library of Australia

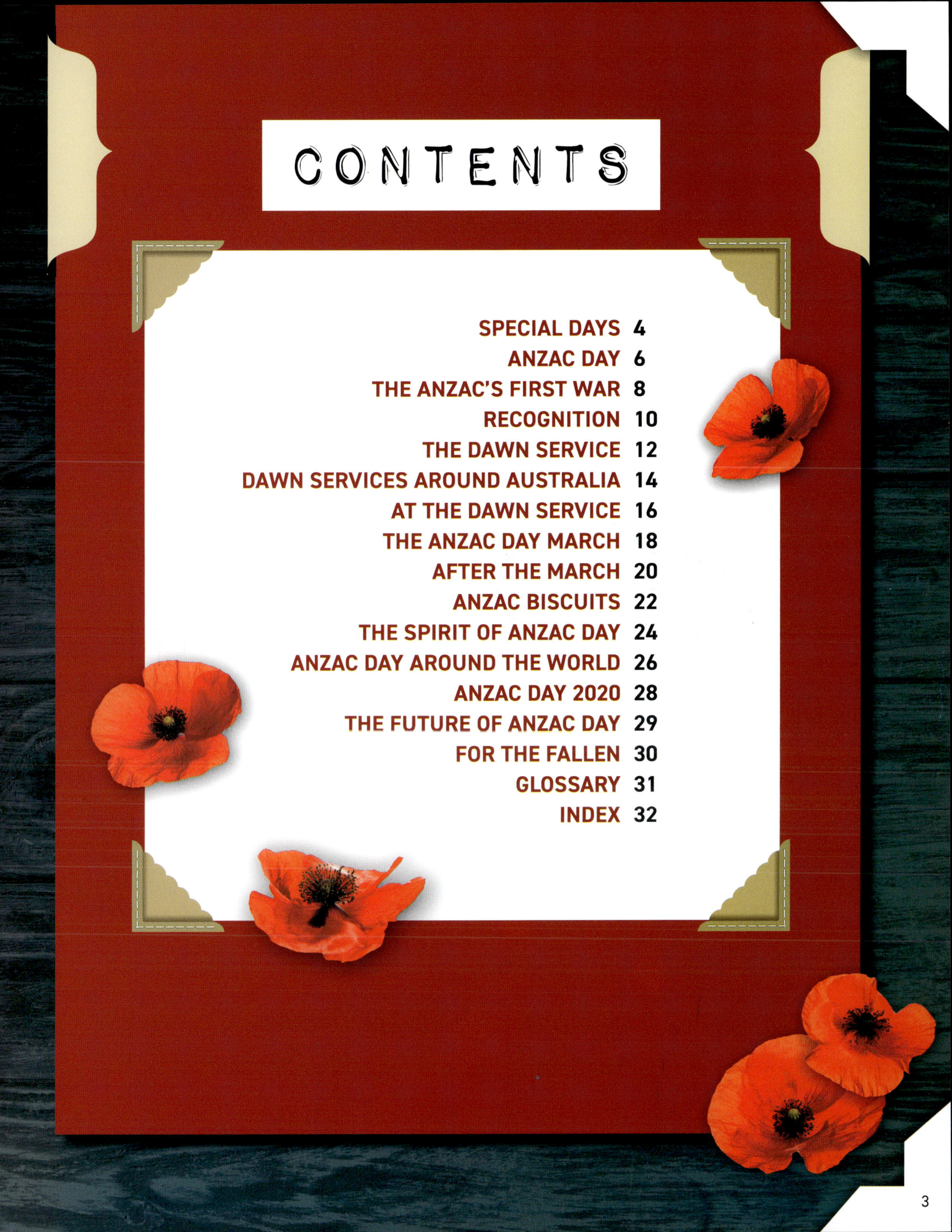

CONTENTS

SPECIAL DAYS

In Australia we celebrate or commemorate a number of special days throughout the year. Some are public holidays, which means people can have the day off work or school. Some special days are marked with events and festivities.

Many special days in Australia commemorate something of historical importance. This gives Australians the opportunity to recognise how people and events have shaped our nation. Australia is a multicultural society with a federation of states and territories. Some special days are significant only to a particular state. Some are important to a specific culture, community or religious group.

Special days are a chance to reflect on the past, to appreciate the world we know, and to look to the future together. On these days, we reflect on the things that make Australia what it is today.

ANZAC DAY

DAY: Anzac Day
DATE: 25 April
WHERE: All states and territories
WHAT: A public holiday that commemorates the service of the Australian and New Zealand Army Corps (ANZAC)

On the 25th of April each year, Australians mark Anzac Day with a public holiday. It is a day when people remember, thank and commemorate all the men and women who have, and still do serve, in the Australian armed forces. Anzac Day reminds us of our hope for all the people of the world to try to live in peace.

IS ANZAC DAY THE SAME AS REMEMBRANCE DAY?

No. Remembrance Day is for remembering all the service men and women who have died since the First World War. Anzac Day is for remembering, commemorating and supporting both past and present Australian and New Zealand Defence Force personnel. Remembrance Day is observed on 11 November. This is the same date that the First World War came to an end and is also known as Armistice Day. Both days are a way of acknowledging the service and sacrifice of our Defence Force personnel.

Anzac Day was originally chosen to commemorate those who fought at Gallipoli. This special day now honours all Australians who served, or still serve, in other wars, conflicts and peacekeeping operations around the world.

DID YOU KNOW?

Anzacs include all defence personnel in the Navy, Army and Air Force who are or were involved in:

- WORLD WAR I
- WORLD WAR II
- THE KOREAN WAR
- THE STABILISATION OF EAST TIMOR
- THE WAR IN AFGHANISTAN
- THE VIETNAM WAR
- THE IRAQ WAR
- THE WAR ON ISIL

THE ANZAC'S FIRST WAR

The Anzac's first battle was in the First World War. This battle began on the dawn of the 25th of April, 1915. That campaign lasted eight months and killed 8,000 men – half of the 16,000 men who landed on the Gallipoli Peninsula at what is now called Anzac Cove.

WHY WERE THE ANZACS SENT TO GALLIPOLI?

The First World War was an effort between Britain and Germany to gain world dominance over the other. Both countries had formed alliances, or sides, with other countries who agreed to support one another with trade and military protection. Both sides also had powerful Empires that included other colonised countries, such as Australia. As part of the British Empire, Australian soldiers joined the war to help Britain secure an important sea trade route. The route runs through the seas between Europe and Asia and was essential for the supply of weapons.

FLAG OF GERMANY

FLAG OF GREAT BRITAIN

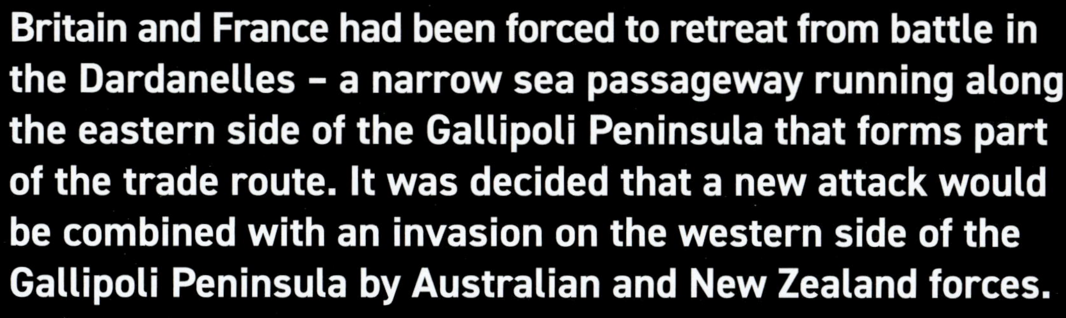

Britain and France had been forced to retreat from battle in the Dardanelles – a narrow sea passageway running along the eastern side of the Gallipoli Peninsula that forms part of the trade route. It was decided that a new attack would be combined with an invasion on the western side of the Gallipoli Peninsula by Australian and New Zealand forces.

The Anzacs sailed from Egypt, where they had been stationed for training, to an island in the Aegean Sea. From there they sailed to Gallipoli, launching their attack at dawn on the 25th of April 1915, at what came to be known as Anzac Cove.

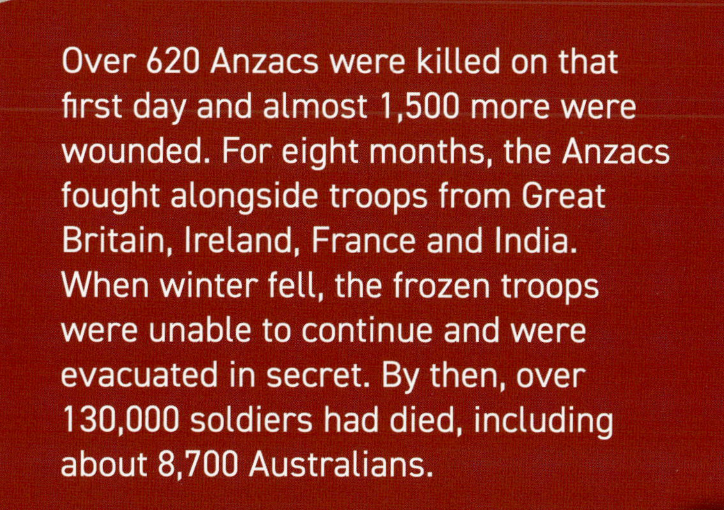

Over 620 Anzacs were killed on that first day and almost 1,500 more were wounded. For eight months, the Anzacs fought alongside troops from Great Britain, Ireland, France and India. When winter fell, the frozen troops were unable to continue and were evacuated in secret. By then, over 130,000 soldiers had died, including about 8,700 Australians.

RECOGNITION

E. S. SMITH, 1916

ABORIGINAL AND TORRES STRAIT ISLANDER ANZACS

Up until 1949, Aboriginal and Torres Strait Islander people were legally excluded from joining the Australian Defence Force because they were not recognised as Australian citizens.

Despite this, it is estimated that over 1,000 Aboriginal and Torres Strait Islander people served in the First World War and a further 8,000 in the Second World War. Those who enlisted were so eager to defend the country they loved, that they hid their racial backgrounds, putting their country before themselves. To this day, the number who served in either war remains an estimate.

For many years, returned Aboriginal and Torres Strait Islander servicemen weren't able to take part in Anzac Day services or gatherings. They were excluded from marches and the special events held afterwards at RSL clubs. These soldiers are only just beginning to be recognised for their service because they were forced to lie about their race. Many also changed their their name and sometimes their date of birth too when enlisting. This makes it very difficult to trace their legacy today.

PRIVATE THOMAS BLACKMANN, 1917

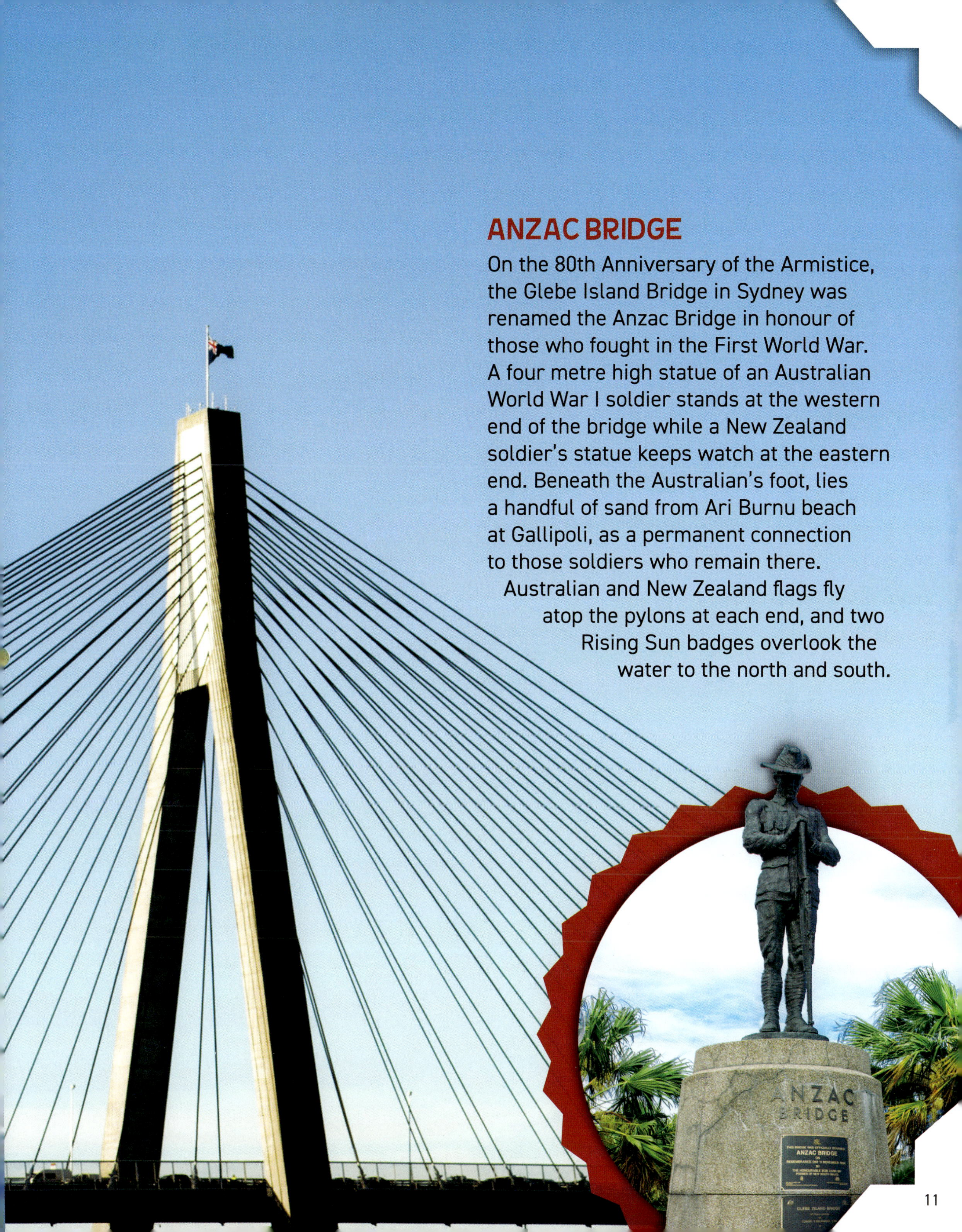

ANZAC BRIDGE

On the 80th Anniversary of the Armistice, the Glebe Island Bridge in Sydney was renamed the Anzac Bridge in honour of those who fought in the First World War. A four metre high statue of an Australian World War I soldier stands at the western end of the bridge while a New Zealand soldier's statue keeps watch at the eastern end. Beneath the Australian's foot, lies a handful of sand from Ari Burnu beach at Gallipoli, as a permanent connection to those soldiers who remain there.

Australian and New Zealand flags fly atop the pylons at each end, and two Rising Sun badges overlook the water to the north and south.

THE DAWN SERVICE

Soldiers on the front line were often called upon to attack the enemy in the half-light of dawn. They were woken in the dark, to be ready to fight at the first glimpse of light. The Dawn Service honours those early morning moments as the soldiers were called to 'stand to'.

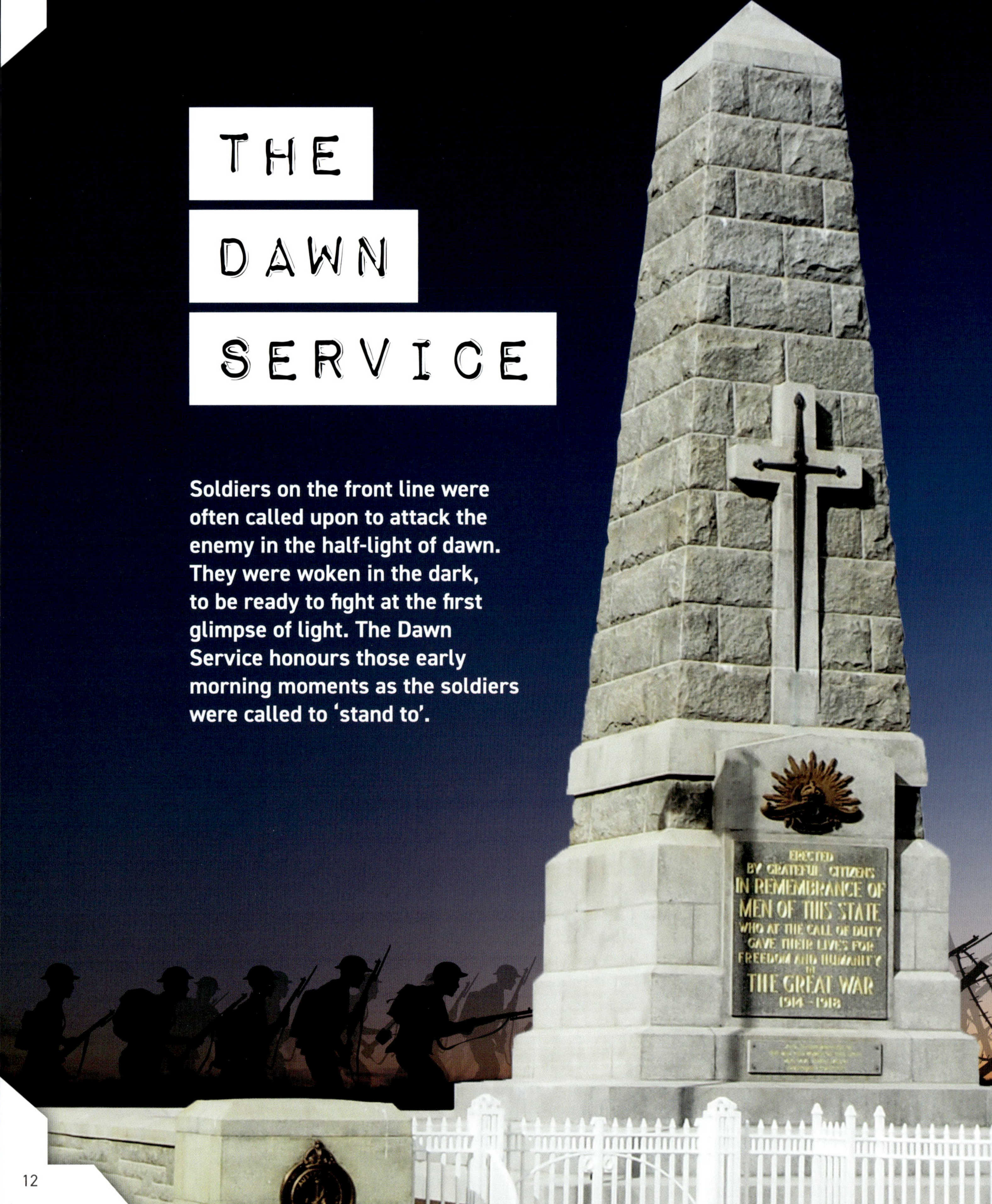

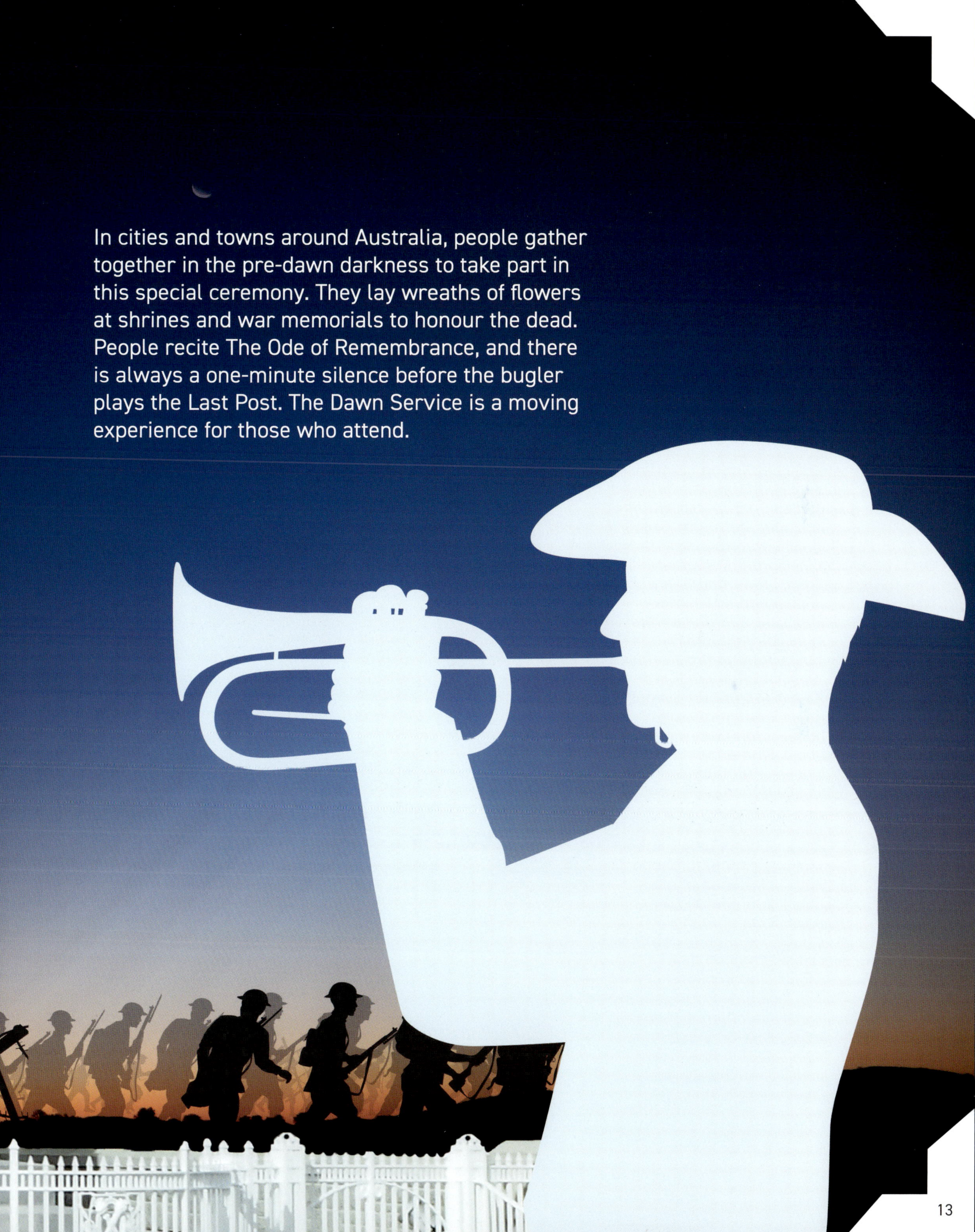

In cities and towns around Australia, people gather together in the pre-dawn darkness to take part in this special ceremony. They lay wreaths of flowers at shrines and war memorials to honour the dead. People recite The Ode of Remembrance, and there is always a one-minute silence before the bugler plays the Last Post. The Dawn Service is a moving experience for those who attend.

DAWN SERVICES AROUND AUSTRALIA

DARWIN, NORTHERN TERRITORY

THE CENOTAPH, BICENTENNIAL PARK

Anzac Day holds special significance in The Northern Territory. In 1942, during the Second World War, Japanese forces bombed Darwin. Every year, people gather at the Cenotaph, which stands on the spot where Australia's first defensive shots were fired. During the service, people look out across the harbour, from where soldiers would leave for war.

PERTH, WESTERN AUSTRALIA

THE CENOTAPH, STATE WAR MEMORIAL PRECINCT, KINGS PARK

Around 40,000 people gather before dawn at Perth's State War Memorial Cenotaph. This 18-metre high obelisk honours all Western Australians who gave their lives in the service of their country. The Flame of Remembrance burns constantly in The State War Memorial Precinct to symbolise the promise, 'We will remember them'.

CURRUMBIN, QUEENSLAND

ELEPHANT ROCK, CURRUMBIN BEACH

The Dawn Service at Elephant Rock is televised nationally with a live cross to commemorations in Gallipoli. The beach location is symbolic of the Gallipoli foreshore and the event attracts thousands of people each year.

MELBOURNE, VICTORIA

THE SHRINE OF REMEMBRANCE, THE KINGS DOMAIN

Melbourne's inner city Anzac Day Service is attended by thousands of people. This televised service begins at 6.00 am.

CANBERRA, AUSTRALIAN CAPITAL TERRITORY

THE AUSTRALIAN WAR MEMORIAL, CAMPBELL

This is the national memorial to all the members of the armed forces who have served and died in wars. The memorial includes a museum, shrine, research centre and library. The original memorial was opened in 1941 to recognise the catastrophic losses Australia suffered during the First World War. Around 50,000 people usually attend the Dawn Service at the Australian War Memorial. In 2015, on the centenary of the Anzac landings at Gallipoli, over 150,000 people attended the service.

SYDNEY, NEW SOUTH WALES

THE CENOTAPH, MARTIN PLACE

This is the state's biggest Anzac Day Service. Thousands of people gather from as early as 3.00 am, for the official service to start at 4.30 am.

AT THE DAWN SERVICE

RECITATION OF THE ODE OF REMEMBRANCE

The Ode of Remembrance is part of a longer poem called *For the Fallen*. It was written by Laurence Binyon in 1914. On Anzac Day, The Ode is recited by one of the special speakers who are invited to tell personal stories or read poems at the Dawn Service. These speakers are usually returned servicemen and servicewomen.

THE ODE

They shall grow not old, as we that are left grow old:
Age shall not weary them, nor the years condemn.
At the going down of the sun and in the morning
We will remember them. *

After the recitation ends, everyone in the audience will reply, *'Lest we forget'.*

*Read the full poem on page 30.

LAYING OF WREATHS

On Anzac Day, we lay wreaths and flowers at memorials in memory of those men and women who lost their lives in the service of their country. Wreaths can be made from a number of different plants and flowers. Traditionally, the use of rosemary symbolises remembrance and the red poppy symbolises the soldier's sacrifice.

BUGLE CALLS

The Last Post is a bugle call first played in the British Army in the late 1700s to mark the end of the day. Over time, it became the bugle call that is played at military funerals to symbolise the end of that soldier's service. On Anzac Day, the Last Post is followed by one or two minutes of silence. A second bugle call, called the 'Reveille', then calls soldiers to 'wake up' and lift their spirits once more.

SILENCE

One or two minutes of silence are included in all Anzac Day Dawn Services. It is a time for everyone gathered to remember and to reflect.

THE ANZAC DAY MARCH

The Anzac Day March is a parade that honours the sacrifices made by defence personnel in the service of their country. It follows the Dawn Service and is watched by thousands of people, both on the streets and at home on television.

Second World War veterans usually lead the march, sometimes supported by their families. They are followed by current defence personnel from the Navy, Army and Air Force. The civilians that support the troops march next, followed by the descendants of any Anzacs that have died during or since active service.

MEDALS

Medals are awarded to Anzacs for their service in conflicts and wars, as well as for recognition of gallantry or distinguished conduct. Those people who served and were awarded the medal wear them on their left breast. Relatives or friends who are marching in honour of a veteran must wear the medals on their right breast.

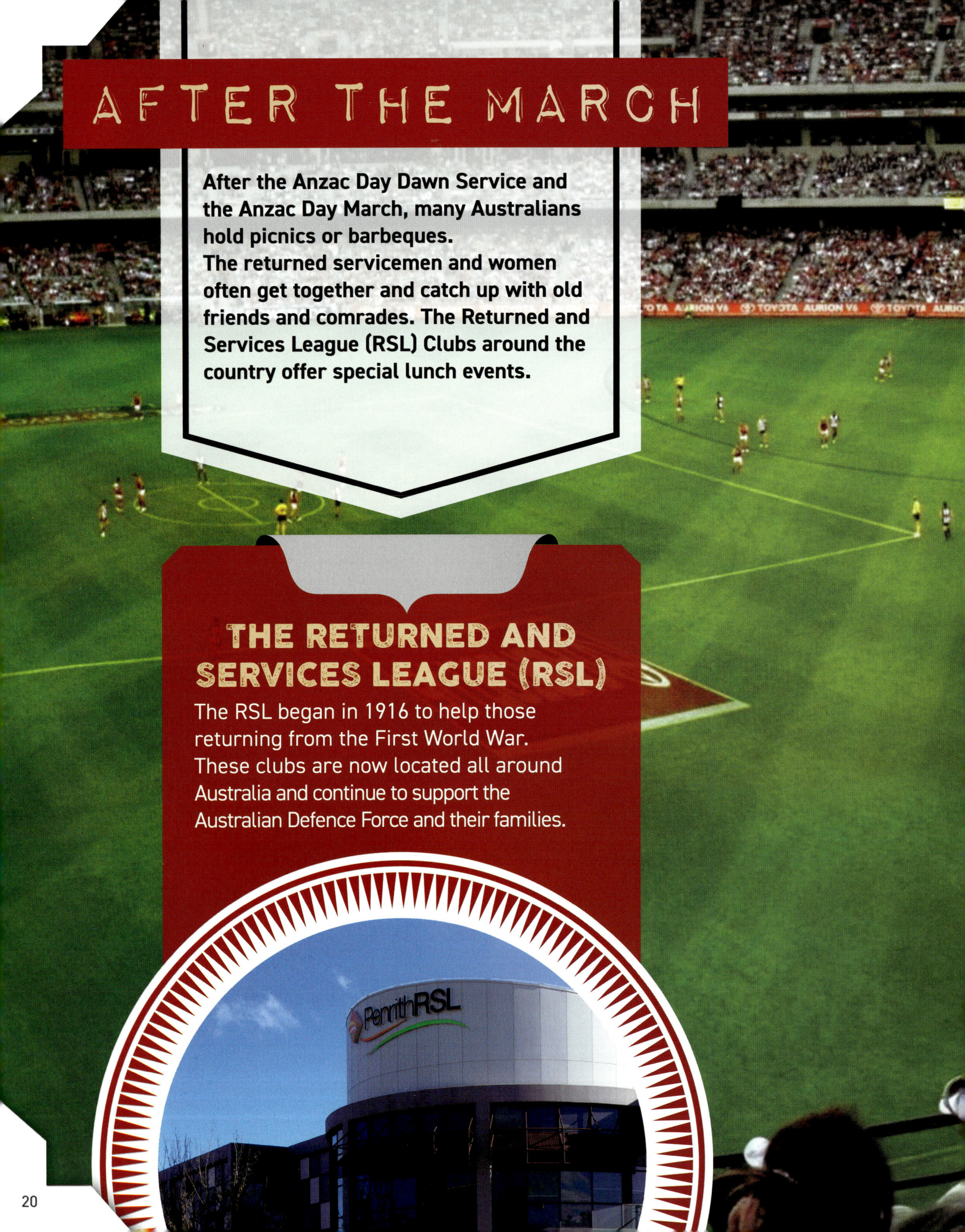

AFTER THE MARCH

After the Anzac Day Dawn Service and the Anzac Day March, many Australians hold picnics or barbeques. The returned servicemen and women often get together and catch up with old friends and comrades. The Returned and Services League (RSL) Clubs around the country offer special lunch events.

THE RETURNED AND SERVICES LEAGUE (RSL)

The RSL began in 1916 to help those returning from the First World War. These clubs are now located all around Australia and continue to support the Australian Defence Force and their families.

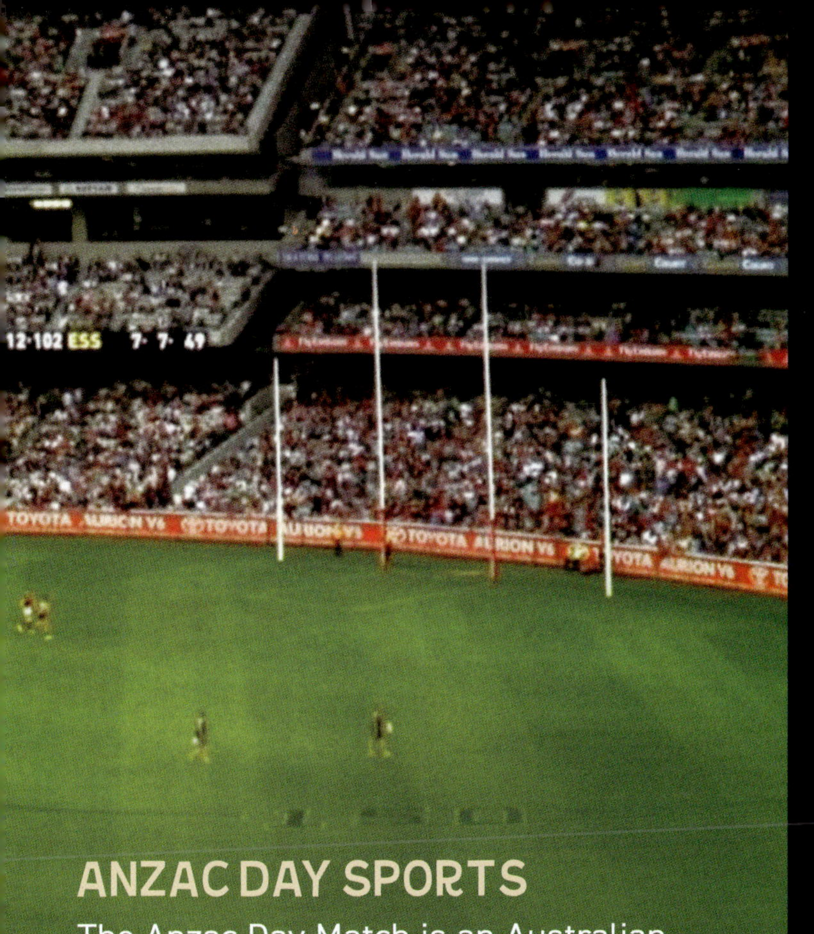

ANZAC DAY SPORTS

The Anzac Day Match is an Australian rules football game between Collingwood and Essendon, held at the Melbourne Cricket Ground (MCG). It follows a special Anzac Day Service at the MCG and includes the playing of the Last Post. In 2002, the NRL introduced the Anzac Day Cup. This is a rugby league game, played between the Sydney Roosters and the St. George Illawarra Dragons, in honour of the Australian and New Zealand Army Corps.

COLLINGWOOD VS ESSENDO, MELBOURNE AUSTRALIA

TWO-UP

In clubs and pubs around the country, Anzac Day traditions include playing two-up. This is a traditional gambling game that involves throwing pennies into the air, to then guess which way up they will land. It is illegal to play two-up except on Anzac Day.

ANZAC BISCUITS

During the First World War, a group of women decided to make biscuits to send to the soldiers that would be nutritious and able to keep from spoiling for a long period of time. The biscuits were made of rolled oats, sugar, flour, coconut, butter and golden syrup. At first they were called soldiers biscuits, but later the name was changed to Anzac biscuits.

DID YOU KNOW?

Today, Anzac biscuits are considered an Australian classic, and are sold in supermarkets all over the country. Many Australian families make their own Anzac biscuits for Anzac Day.

RECIPE

INGREDIENTS

1 cup of plain flour
1 cup of rolled oats
1 cup of brown sugar
1/2 cup of coconut
125 grams of unsalted butter
2 tablespoons of golden syrup
1/2 tablespoon of bicarbonate of soda
1 tablespoon of water

METHOD

Preheat oven at 175°C.

Grease or line a baking tray with baking paper.

Sift the flour into a bowl and then add the sugar, rolled oats and coconut.

In a saucepan, melt the butter and then add golden syrup, water and bicarbonate of soda.

Add the liquid mixture to the dry ingredients and mix thoroughly.

Press the mixture into biscuits and place on the tray.

Bake for 15-20 minutes.

Cool the biscuits until they harden.

Store in an airtight container.

THE SPIRIT OF ANZAC DAY

The Australian soldiers who served in the First World War were known for their loyalty and mateship. Helping your mates is important, and during wartime many Australian soldiers risked their lives for their mates. This courage, along with a sense of humour as they faced harrowing conditions, illness and danger came to be known as Anzac spirit. Many books, films and stories focus on the Anzac spirit as an important result of the war. It is a spirit that lives on in Australians today.

SIMPSON AND HIS DONKEY

One of the most well-known Anzacs was Private John Simpson from the Australian Army Medical Corps, who used a donkey called Duffy to help carry wounded soldiers to safety. Private Simpson only served in Gallipoli for one month. He was killed in action on 19 May 1915, aged just 22 years old.